TEACH YOURSELF

W9-AAS-063

Bluegrass
Mandolin

by Andy Statman

Teach yourself authentic bluegrass. Clear instructions from a professional; basics,
right- and left-hand techniques, solos, backup, personal advice on performance and much more.
Plus a complete selection of the best bluegrass songs and tunes to learn from.

Cover photography of mandolin by Randall Wallace
Background cover photography by Herb Wise
Project editors: Peter Pickow and Ed Lozano
Musical contractor: Bob Grant
Interior design and layout: Don Giller

This book Copyright © 1978 by Amsco Publications,
A Division of Music Sales Corporation, New York
This edition published 1999 by Oak Publications,
A Division of Embassy Music Corporation, New York

Order No. OK 64994
US International Standard Book Number: 0.8256.0326.9
UK International Standard Book Number: 0.7119.7623.6

Exclusive Distributors:
Music Sales Corporation
257 Park Avenue South, New York, NY 10010 USA
Music Sales Limited
8/9 Frith Street, London W1V 5TZ England
Music Sales Pty. Limited
120 Rothschild Street, Rosebery, Sydney, NSW 2018, Australia

Printed in the United States of America by
Vicks Lithograph and Printing Corporation

Oak Publications
New York/London/Paris/Sydney/Copenhagen/Madrid

Compact Disc Track Listing

CD Personnel

Bob Grant: Mandolin, Guitar, and Vocals
Tony Trischka: Banjo
Antoine Silverman: Fiddle
Matt Weiner: Bass

Table of Contents

Introduction

Bluegrass is an exciting musical idiom that developed in the South in the mid-1940s. It combined elements as seemingly diverse as the blues and Scottish fiddle tunes into a wonderful, new musical form. Bill Monroe, a tenor singer and mandolin player from Kentucky, served as the focal point for the development of this new music. His high, powerful voice soared over the exciting rhythm he played on the mandolin. His style of mandolin playing was "hotter" than anything anyone had ever heard. Soon other bands began following in his footsteps. Each band and player had an important contribution to make. The disc jockeys called this new musical form bluegrass, after Bill Monroe's band, the Blue Grass Boys. Some thirty years later this music is still alive and growing.

The mandolin is an essential part of a bluegrass band. It comes from an ancient family of double-stringed instruments that includes the oud, one of the older brothers of the mandolin. These instruments originated in Central Asia and the Middle East. In time, the oud and other related instruments filtered into southern Europe. Many of them were unsuitable for European music. They did, however, provide the model for the mandolin.

The mandolin originated in either Spain or Italy. In Italy, there were several versions of the instrument, each differing in its number of strings. However, the Neapolitan-style mandolin (four double strings) became the most popular, spreading throughout Europe and eventually reaching the Americas. A favorite instrument of the late 1890s and early 1900s, it founded a comfortable home in the traditional music of the southern mountains of the United States.

Most of the mandolins in use then were round backs or "tater bugs." However, in time, mandolins with flat backs began to be produced. The Gibson Company, founded around the turn of the century, made some of the best. These flat-backed mandolins, especially the F5 Artist Model, found great favor among bluegrass musicians. Today they're sought after and highly prized.

Now . . . do you need a rare Gibson with which to play bluegrass? No. Any mandolin (Harmony, Stradolin, Martin, etc.) will do, providing it's in good shape. I've seen many less expensive mandolins that sound as good as, if not better than, those that cost a fortune. Don't let convention sway you. A good mandolin is a good mandolin, no matter what the make.

For bluegrass, flat-back mandolins are preferable because they project better. However, if you have one with a round back, it will do fine. Mandolins have either F or round holes. The harder sound of the F hole is preferred by many bluegrass musicians. The mellower sounding round hole can work just as well. Choose whichever sounds best to you.

The purpose of this book is to acquaint you with the basics of bluegrass mandolin. It will teach you how to get that bluegrass sound. Go through the book slowly and absorb each new idea before you move on to the next. Sometimes you'll get bogged down, but don't get discouraged. It's best not to force the learning process. Let the troublesome part rest for a few days, and come back to it later. You may then find it easier to do.

As you learn new techniques, go back and apply them to tunes you learned earlier. The more you learn and play, the more you will realize that there are common phrases that continually reappear. At that point, you will have begun to learn the music language of bluegrass.

But there is only so much you can learn from a book. Listen to recordings and go to live concerts whenever you can. Try to find other musicians to play with. This is probably the most valuable thing you can do. It will teach you to apply what you've learned to a real situation.

As you develop, don't be scared to take chances or try new ideas. Express yourself. The mandolin is an extension of your body and soul, and a vehicle with which to express your emotions and thoughts.

I hope this book turns you on to the beauties of bluegrass mandolin. Enjoy yourself!

Holding the Mandolin

Hold the mandolin tilted slightly upwards. When you play sitting down, use your thigh (preferably the right one) and torso for support.

When you play standing up, use a strap. It will support the mandolin and allow you to move your hands more freely. The length of the strap determines where the mandolin rests next to your body. Too high or low a placement can hurt your playing by making it harder for your hands and fingers to move. The mandolin is best placed between your waist and chest. Put it where it suits you.

The strap can be made of strong string, a leather cord, two shoelaces, dental floss, and so on. Attach it by pushing one end of the cord between the strings and the headstock, next to the nut. Loop this end around the neck and tie. Then attach the other end at the tail pin. Make sure the tail pin is secure and the knots are tightly tied. On a mandolin with a scroll, the strap can be looped through the scroll and tied.

Tuning

The mandolin is tuned by tightening or loosening the tuning pegs. Each pair of strings is tuned in unison as follows:

EE: First string, thinnest, highest in pitch

AA: Second string, slightly thicker, second highest in pitch

DD: Third string, wound, lower in pitch

GG: Fourth string, thickest and wound, lowest in pitch.

Here are few easy tuning methods.

The Pitch Pipe

Ask your music store for a mandolin (or violin) pitch pipe. These pipes are pre-tuned to the exact pitch of each set of strings. Start by blowing gently into the highest-sounding pipe and tune your E strings to it. Then tune the other pairs of strings to the remaining pipes. Beware, though: after prolonged use, the pitch of the pipes may become inaccurate.

The Tuning Fork

I prefer the tuning fork to the pitch pipe because it stays in tune for a longer period of time. Purchase a fork that is tuned to A or 440 (the number of vibrations per second). Strike the fork against a hard surface and place the tail of it on the top of the bridge of the mandolin.

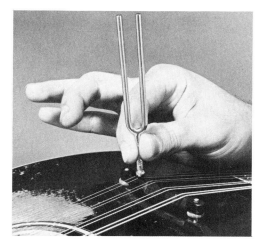

This will produce an A to which you can tune your second set of strings. Now you can get the rest of the strings in tune by means of fret tuning.

Fret Tuning

Once your A strings are in tune, the rest of the mandolin can be tuned by the following method. Fret the A string at the seventh fret. The note produced is the correct pitch of the open E string. After turning the E string to this pitch, fret the D string at the seventh fret. Tune the D strings until they are the same pitch as the open A strings. Then do the same for the G strings. Fret them at the seventh fret and tune them until their pitch is the same as that of the open D strings.

When the mandolin is out of tune with itself you can use this method to tune quickly. Remember: any string fretted on the seventh fret is equal in pitch to the open string placed below it on the neck.

The Piano

You can also tune your mandolin to a piano. The following diagram will show how the open strings correspond to the notes on the keyboard.

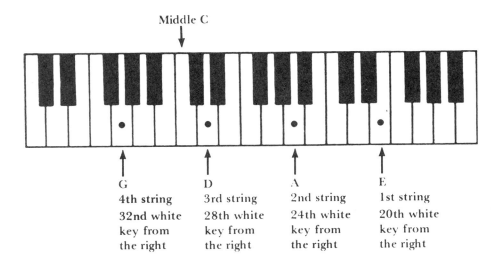

Middle C

G	D	A	E
4th string	**3rd string**	**2nd string**	**1st string**
32nd white key from the right	28th white key from the right	24th white key from the right	20th white key from the right

Once you've tuned by any of the above methods, check again to make sure all the strings are still in tune. Strings expand and contract during tuning and you may have to re-tune (fine tune).

Notation

Time Value

The notes you play are held for different lengths of time. We will use the following method to notate this time value.

Tap your foot at a moderate tempo. With each tap, count aloud: one-two-three-four. Each of these beats equals a quarter note. This is shown by:

Quarter Note

Continue tapping your foot at the same tempo. When your foot hits the ground, say *one, and* when your foot is raised, say *and.* You are now counting eighth notes, one-and-two-and-three-and-four-and. Eighth notes are notated like this:

Eighth Notes

Occasionally you will be using sixteenth and thirty-second notes. Two sixteenth notes are equal to one eighth note. Two thirty-second notes are equal in value to one sixteenth note. They appear on the staff like this:

Sixteenth Note and
Thirty-Second Note

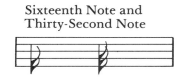

Two larger note values we encounter are the whole note, equal in time value to four quarter notes; and the half note, equal to two quarter notes. This is how they are notated:

Half Note   Whole Note

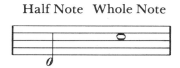

At times while you're playing, you will pause or rest for a given amount of time that corresponds to a whole note, a half note, etc. The length of these rests are indicated as follows:

Rests
Whole Half   Quarter Eighth Sixteenth

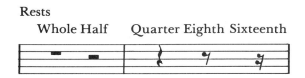

A triplet is a series of three notes of equal time value, played in the space of a quarter or an eighth note, as designated:

Sometimes part of a song is repeated. When you see the following symbol, go back to the beginning and start again.

Repeat

In some cases you will play a second ending that is different from the first. This is notated like this:

First + Second Endings

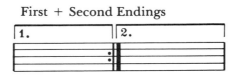

This means that you play through the first ending and repeat the section. This time, skip the first ending and play only the second.

The notes are placed on a staff made up of five horizontal lines separated by four spaces. A vertical line drawn across the staff is called a barline. The space between two barlines is called a bar or measure. Two parallel lines at the end of a measure indicate the end of a section or piece.

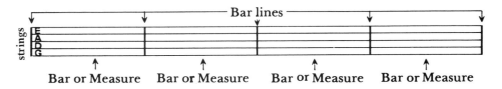

Although the rhythmic pattern may vary from bar to bar, the total playing time of each bar will remain the same.

The time signature tells the meter of a tune and is written in the first bar. The time signature is notated as a fraction without the line in the middle. These are the time signatures you will play in throughout this book:

Time Signatures

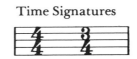

The top number tells you how many beats (counts) there are in a measure. The bottom number tells you the kind of notes that receive one beat.

For example:

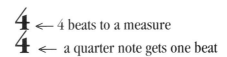
$\frac{4}{4}$ ← 4 beats to a measure
← a quarter note gets one beat

The measure can contain any combination of notes and rests as long as they add up to the time signature. In the above example, each measure can contain notes and rests that together add up to a total of four quarter notes.

You can better understand some of the things we've talked about by playing this specially adapted version of *Old MacDonald's Farm.*

Old MacDonald's Farm

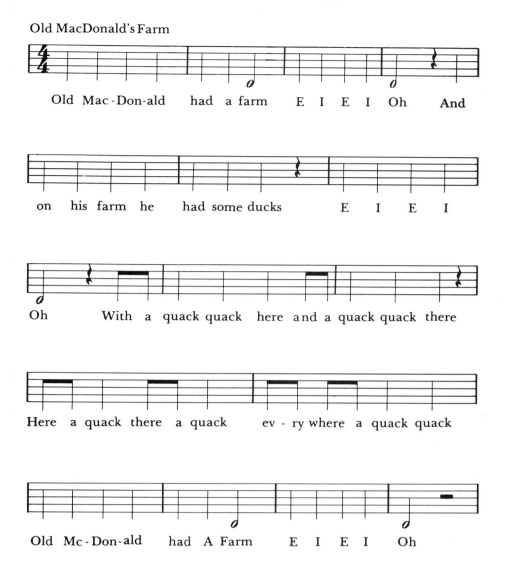

Old Mac-Don-ald   had a farm   E   I   E   I   Oh   And

on   his farm   he   had some ducks   E   I   E   I

Oh   With   a   quack quack   here and a quack quack there

Here   a quack there   a   quack   ev - ry where a quack quack

Old Mc-Don-ald   had A Farm   E   I   E   I   Oh

Tablature

Tablature is a simplified form of musical notation. Its staff is composed of five horizontal lines.

Each open space between two lines represents a string on the mandolin. The number written in that space indicates at what fret the given string is to be fretted. The first string fretted at the third fret would look like this:

When you play an open string it is indicated like this:

When two or more strings are to be played simultaneously they appear in tablature like this:

Occasionally you will slide into a note from a lower or higher fret. The first number indicates at what fret the slide begins and the second number tells you where the slide ends. You pick the string only once on the first number. Then slide to the second. The slide is completed in the given time value.

Other Tablature Symbols

When two strings are played and one of them has a slide:

When you slide on two strings simultaneously:

An up-stroke or upward movement of the pick:

A down-stroke or downward movement of the pick:

A tremolo:

Sometimes certain notes are accented or played louder than others:

Hammering-on is an easy technique in which you pick a string and then plunk down a finger of the left hand on a higher fret of the same string.

When you hammer-on and then quickly remove the hammered finger, leaving the original note to sound, it is called a hammer-on-and-off. These three notes are produced by one stroke of the pick and are equal in time value to a triplet.

A pull-off is when a string is plucked by a finger of the left hand, sounding either a fretted or open string, as indicated:

Small, circled numbers written above the staff indicate what finger is to be used when playing a given note.

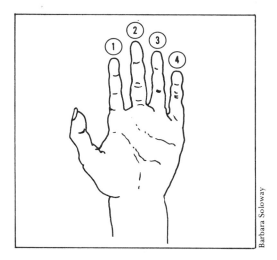

Barbara Soloway

Basic Playing Techniques

Picks

There are many different styles of picks on the market. The different strengths and shapes produce different tones. They come in various sizes and are usually made of plastic or tortoiseshell.

Most bluegrass players prefer the sound of a hard, medium-size pick. There are, of course, exceptions. For instance, Bill Monroe sometimes uses a large tortoiseshell pick. On the other hand, Jesse McReynolds has been known to use a softer, medium-size, plastic pick. In the other styles, such as classical and Russian folk music, players prefer small, hard tortoiseshell picks.

In addition to tortoiseshell and plastic picks, other materials have been used. In the ongoing quest for an ever harder pick, I've seen everything in use from sanded poker chips to rounded pieces of ivory and stone. These rather unusual picks are highly endorsed by their users.

Along with different pick styles and strengths, you can also vary your tone and attack by using either the rounded or pointed end of the pick. Some players go all the way and play with completely round picks. Bobby Osborne and Ronnie Reno do this by taking a large-size, hard, plastic pick, taping it to a quarter, and filing it down until they have a round, quarter-size pick. They sand the rough edges until they are smooth. These picks, which are excellent for bluegrass, give you added punch because with a rounded playing edge, there is less give when the pick hits the strings than there is with a pointed edge. Another advantage is that the playing area of the pick is increased from one small point to the entire pick. These picks, in addition to their value to the musician, make for great slugs and are commonly in use at laundromats, subways, and phone booths!

As you can see, different picks are suited to different styles, and it is up to you to discover what works best. To begin with, though, I recommend a hard, medium-size pick (Fender heavy guitar style). After you've been picking a while and are familiar with the different playing styles, being to experiment with some of the pick styles mentioned above. Choose the pick that gives you the best tone and maximum playing speed and accuracy. However, once you've decided upon a pick, won't worry; proper right-hand technique and development will allow you to play all the styles equally well.

Holding the Pick

Because nobody's right hand is exactly the same, everybody holds the pick in a slightly different way. It is held between your thumb and index finger. Never use your middle finger for added support.

Hold your hand in a loose, open fist. Now, place your thumb on the edge of the index finger at the first joint. The pick lies between these two fingers. The exact placement of the thumb will be slightly different for each person. Whatever you find is most comfortable and provides the best support should be used.

Hold the pick loosely but securely, in a relaxed manner. Rest your thumb gently but firmly on top of the pick.

To prevent your pick from slipping, take a knife or nail file and scratch vertical and horizontal lines in a busy tic-tac-toe pattern onto the center of the pick. This will give you a firmer grip.

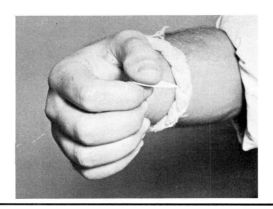

Playing Melody or Lead

In melody or lead playing most of the movement should come from your wrist. Use short, solid, up- and down-strokes. (Occasionally, for musical emphasis, you can play a series of down-strokes.) The strokes should be fluid and relaxed. Take care to produce a clear-sounding note. Your wrist movement should be strong, yet relaxed and unencumbered. A free, loose wrist will give you power, volume, and accuracy. Work to develop equal strength and authority in your up- and down-strokes.

The angle at which the pick hits the strings varies slightly from player to player. It should lie somewhere between being parallel to the strings and at a 20-degree angle (the back of the pick raised).

In playing lead, and also in most rhythm playing, the underside of the forearm rests on the edge of the mandolin (on the binding), just above the tailpiece, for support.

For additional support, some players anchor their ring or pinky finger (or both) on the face of the mandolin, in front of the bridge. This can aid in the accurate execution of difficult passages but may impair speed, fluidity, and tone. Use this method with caution.

Your right hand is responsible for bringing out the tone that lies within the mandolin; you should always be conscious of that tone. Go for a strong, ringing sound that is rich and clear. Make your mandolin "speak."

When you strike the strings close to the bridge, the tone will be hard and sharp. However, when you move away from the bridge, the strings will produce a softer, more mellow sound.

Bill Monroe usually plays close to the bridge, it becomes harder to move your pick and you may slow yourself down. The tone you'll produce there will be tinny and plucky. For the best results, I suggest that you begin by playing about one and a half to two inches from the bridge. Then as you develop, you'll find the area best suited to your taste.

Listen to all the different mandolin players and try to reproduce the tone color of the ones you like. In addition to the different traditional bluegrass tones, experiment to see what new sounds you can get out of your instrument. Don't disregard any of them, no matter how unusual they appear to be. They can be used to good advantage. This experimenting will make you more aware and sensitive to tone color and its application. However, when you find yourself in a conservative bluegrass setting, it's best to stick to the "proper" tone.

The Left Hand

Your left hand supports the neck of the mandolin. The neck should rest between the base of your index finger and the pad of the thumb (with the thumb angles towards the headstock). Leave a space between the hand and neck; don't push the neck back so that it touches the circular area between the thumb and index finger. The thumb acts as a moving anchor, supplying support for the other fingers with which to note. Be sure not to let your thumb extend far above the neck or to bend down far over the neck. If necessary, allow only a small portion of the thumb (a little past the first joint) to extend over the neck. Your fingers should be arched.

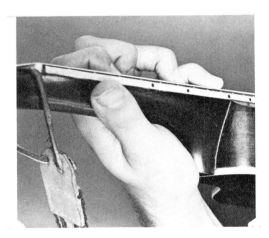

The string is noted by pressing the tip of your finger down on it, just behind the fret. This should be done firmly enough to produce a clean note. Don't press too hard: this will create tension in your left hand and slow down its movement.

The tips of your fingers may hurt in the beginning but calluses will eventually form and the pain will be gone. Bear with it! Your fingers will build up strength, speed and accuracy.

Chords and Playing Rhythm

Chords

Chords are groups of three or more notes played simultaneously. Here are two of the basic bluegrass chords. Try to play them.

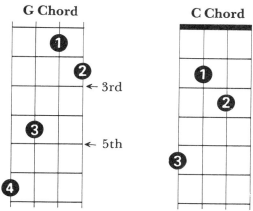

The big G chord may give you trouble with its large reach. Be patient. As your third and fourth fingers gain strength, you'll be able to play it. Press down hard enough to produce clear-sounding notes.

Here are four more chords.

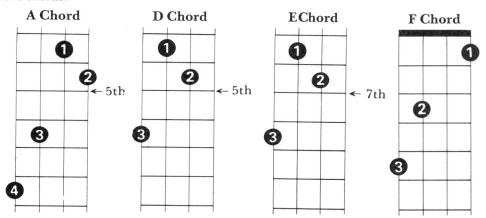

Notice that the A chord fingering is the same as the G chord, except that it is played two frets higher. Also, observe how the C chord becomes a D and then an E chord when moved up the appropriated number of frets. You can use either of these G or C chord positions to make any major chord by moving to the proper fret.

Here are several minor chords. Learn them.

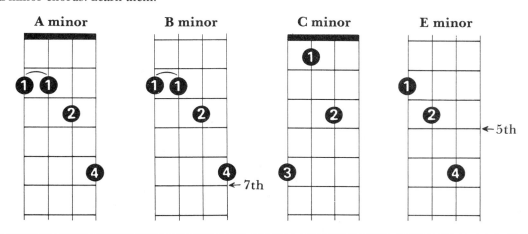

You can make any minor chord if you move these positions to the proper fret.

Seventh chords provide a smooth and bluesy-sounding way to move from one chord into another. Here are some. Try to learn them.

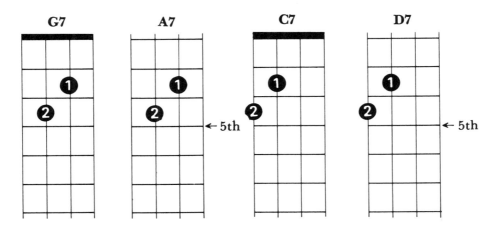

Notice how the index finger can remain stationary when shifting from the major to the seventh chord. A seventh chord can be made in any key by moving this position to the appropriate fret.

Now let's try these chords in *Lonesome Road Blues* and see how they sound. As I've previously mentioned, these chords provide a natural bridge between the other major chords. Use seventh chords wherever you feel they work.

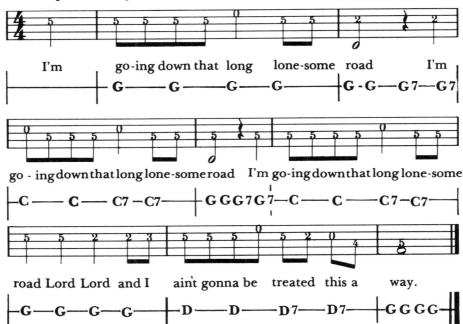

Strum Each Chord Once As Listed - Their Time Value
Equals One Quarter Note

Playing Rhythm

In addition to playing lead, you will also be an integral part of the rhythm section of a bluegrass band. In this role the mandolin can drive and push the band much in the same way a snare drum drives a rock band. Good rhythm playing can generate as much excitement as lead playing, and in so doing, spark the band to a higher level of performance. For this reason, it's up to you to keep good, solid time for the band by laying down a strong, driving rhythm. Your rhythm playing should also complement and respond to vocals or solos.

Being a good rhythm player will greatly improve your lead playing by strengthening your wrist and giving you a better sense of pulse and timing. It will also teach you the rhythmic subtleties inherent in bluegrass music.

Listen to the way the rhythm is played or "chunked" by your favorite mandolinists. Be conscious of the sound they get and how they use the rhythm to keep the band moving.

Your best bet is to listen to Bill Monroe, because he invented the bluegrass style of rhythm mandolin playing. This rhythm style was one of the main innovations that contributed to the development of bluegrass. Its bouncy yet powerful feel differed from previous forms of country music and opened up new ideas for the musician to explore.

These rhythmic innovations gave the player a greater freedom in his or her choice of notes and the way in which they can be used. As a rule, new rhythmic conceptions develop before, and are what make possible, the melodic and harmonic changes that follow.

Let's explore this new rhythm and try to play it. This basic bluegrass mandolin rhythm is played on the upbeats, or on the second and fourth beats of a measure: one-TWO-three-FOUR. The stroke is sharp and percussive and lasts about the length of a quarter note. It should pop. Here's how it looks in tablature:

After you've struck the strings, release the pressure of the left-hand fingers so that they just rest on top of the strings. This stops the ringing and helps create more of a pop.

Your wrist movement should be loose, yet strong. Your forearm should move up and down, giving added power and emphasis to your wrist movement. Make sure you keep your wrist loose and moving freely when the forearm is in motion.

Occasionally you will use your entire arm, moving from the shoulder, along with the wrist and forearm. Your arm pushes down and towards the neck, and helps add extra emphasis and urgency to your rhythm playing.

There are other ways of playing the simple rhythm we learned before. Here's a slightly more developed way of playing it.

A further development of this rhythm is:

Be sure to get the accents correct. Without them, the pattern loses its effectiveness.

Here's an excellent exercise that will help you develop all that we've just talked about. Get hold of some bluegrass recordings and figure out the chords of the tunes that you like. Then play the recordings and chunk along with them. Try the different rhythmic patterns to see how they work and where each is most effective. Be aware of how the mandolin functions as an integral part of the band. Aside from developing your sense of rhythm playing, it will also increase your repertoire.

The Tremolo

One of the most characteristic sounds of the mandolin is the tremolo. The tremolo allows the sound of the mandolin to be sustained naturally. It consists of a rapid series of up and down strokes played on one or more sets of strings.

Commonly associated with popular Italian mandolin playing (*O Sole Mio; Santa Lucia*), the tremolo has found wide use in bluegrass and old-time music. The tremolo can be warm and serene or chilling and exciting. It's particularly effective on slow and medium-tempo songs.

The tremolo should be steady and even. It should also bring out the tone of the mandolin.

Here is a good exercise for developing your tremolo. Tap your foot at a medium tempo and play:

Now double this:

Now double this:

Slowly work up to the faster pick tempos. You'll soon be able to produce a smooth, even tremolo. The speed of the tremolo should be determined by your own musical sense.

There are many fine recorded examples of tremolo playing. Bill Monroe's strong, powerful tremolo provides an excellent model from which to learn. Other good examples have been recorded by Frank Wakefield, Earl Taylor, Earl Bolick (Blue Sky Boys), and David Grisman.

The Tunes

The fingerings used in playing the mandolin are not arbitrary. They're based on the most economical way to reach a note. In order to understand the proper fingering of the first few tunes, you should learn to play the following A and D scales. The interval (space) between the first and last note of a completed scale equals an octave.

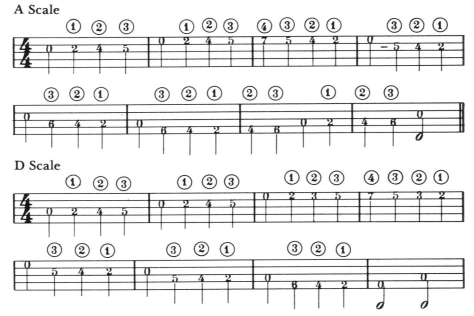

As you can see, certain fingers are used to reach particular notes.

Cripple Creek

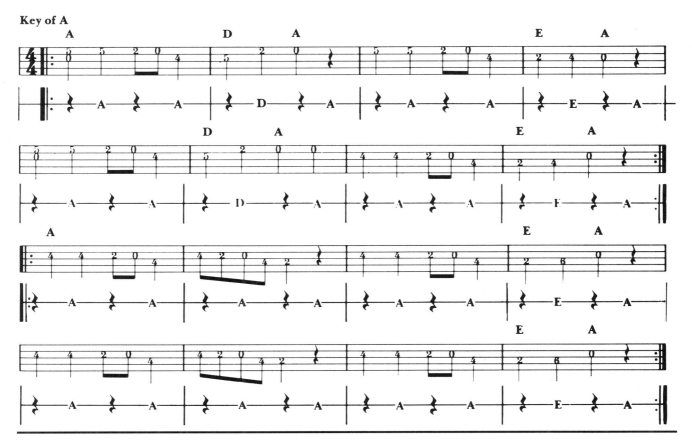

Cripple Creek

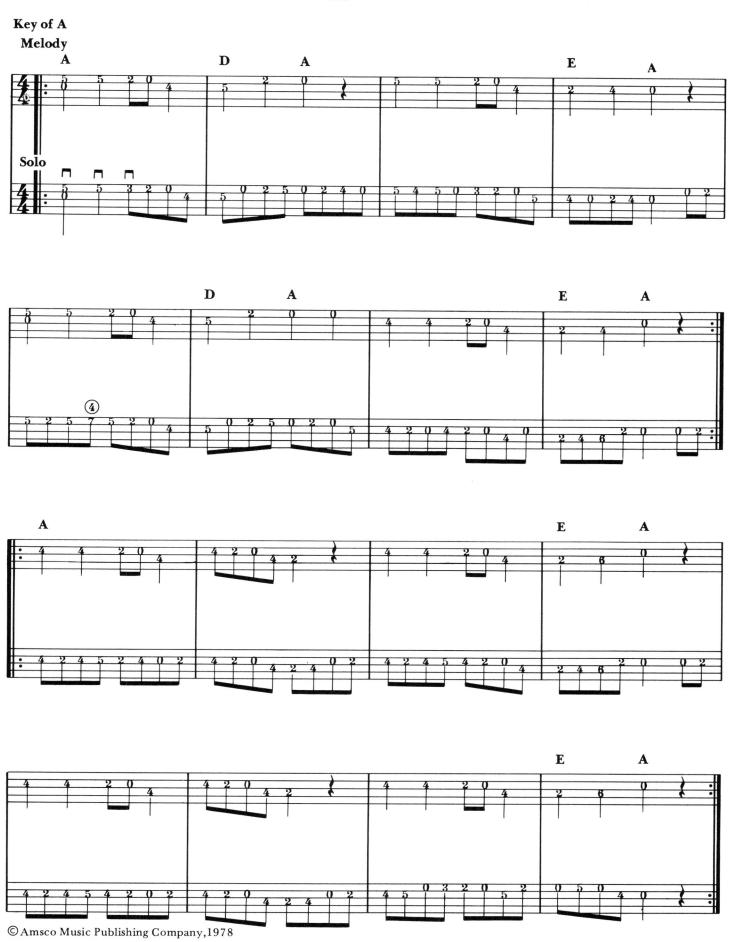

In *Sally Goodin* we start work on the lower strings. In the first bar of the second part we also encounter our first slide. This slide is played simultaneously with an open string.

Sally Goodin

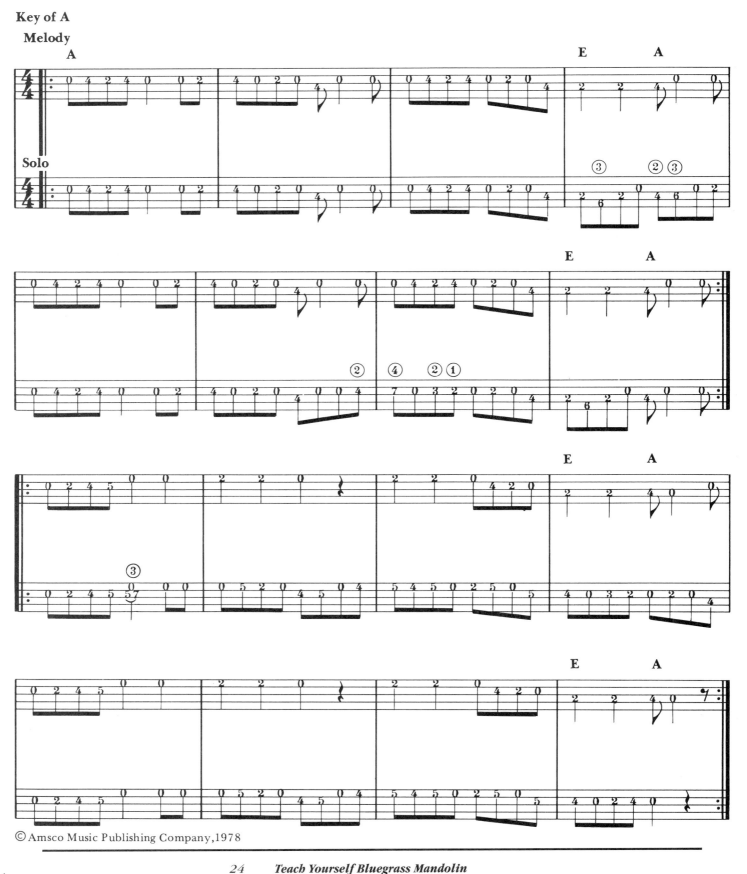

Soldier's Joy

Key of D

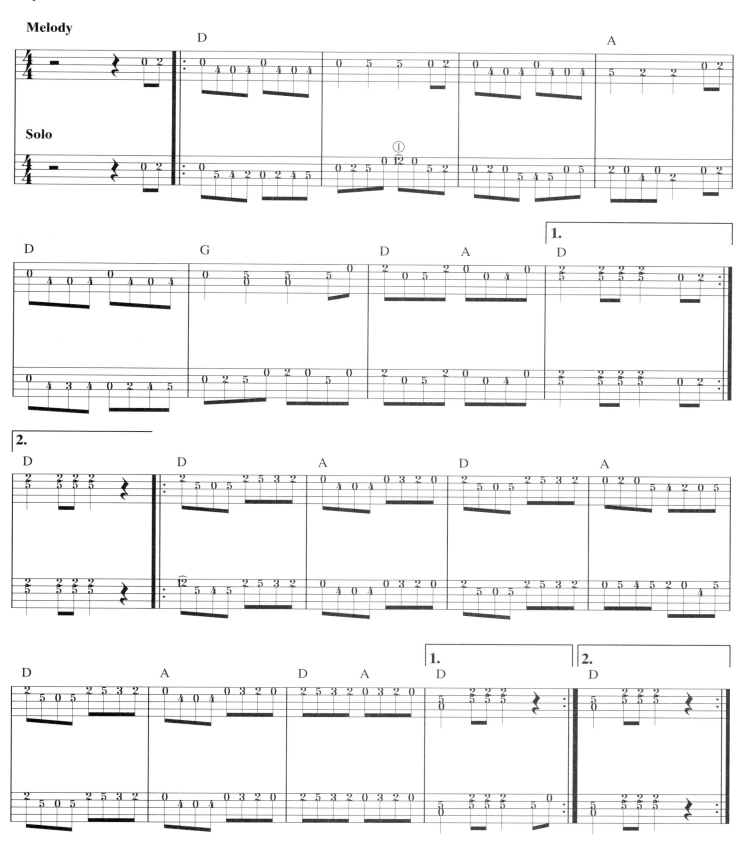

In *Old Joe Clark* and *Salt Creek* we find an important bluegrass rhythm. This rhythm consists of an eighth note played with a down-stroke, a heavily accented quarter note on an up-stroke, an eighth note on an upstroke, and an eighth note on the downstroke. This rhythm is used both in melody and rhythmic backup.

Old Joe Clark

Old Joe Clark

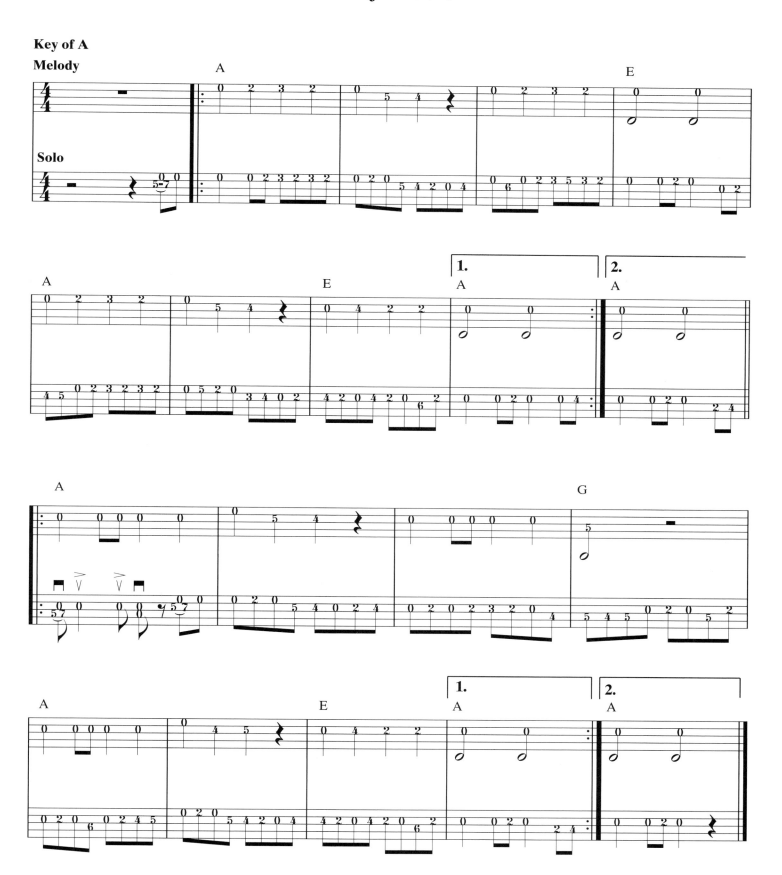

Salt Creek

Key of A

Bill Monroe and Bradford Keith

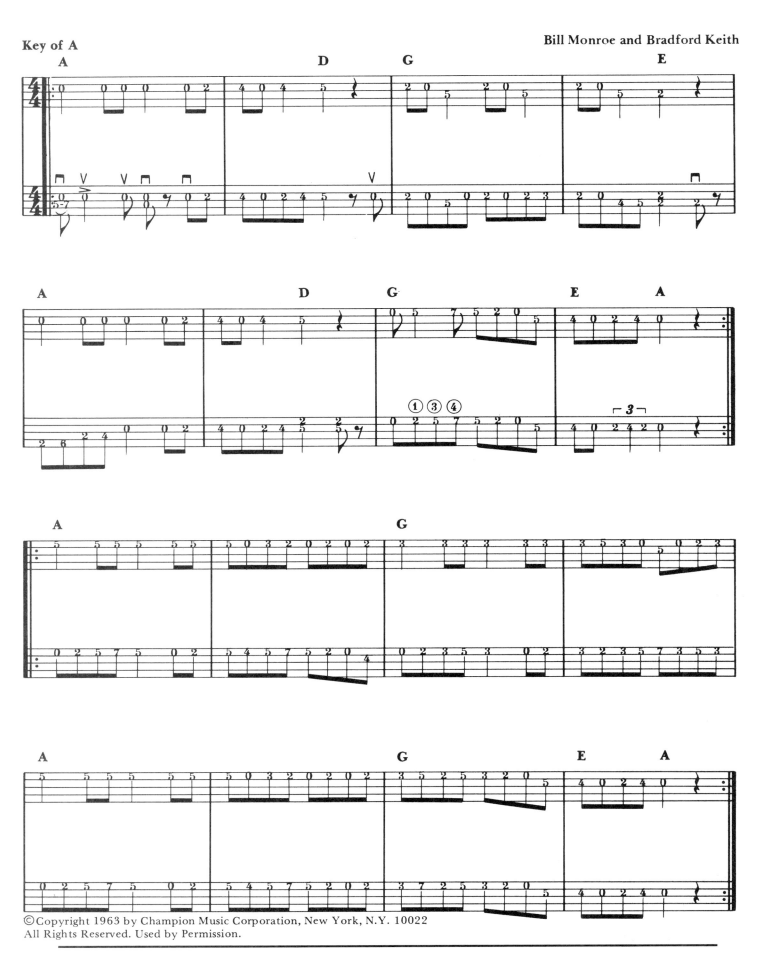

Arkansas Traveller is a tune familiar to everyone. The solo version is played an octave higher than the original.

Arkansas Traveller

Key of D

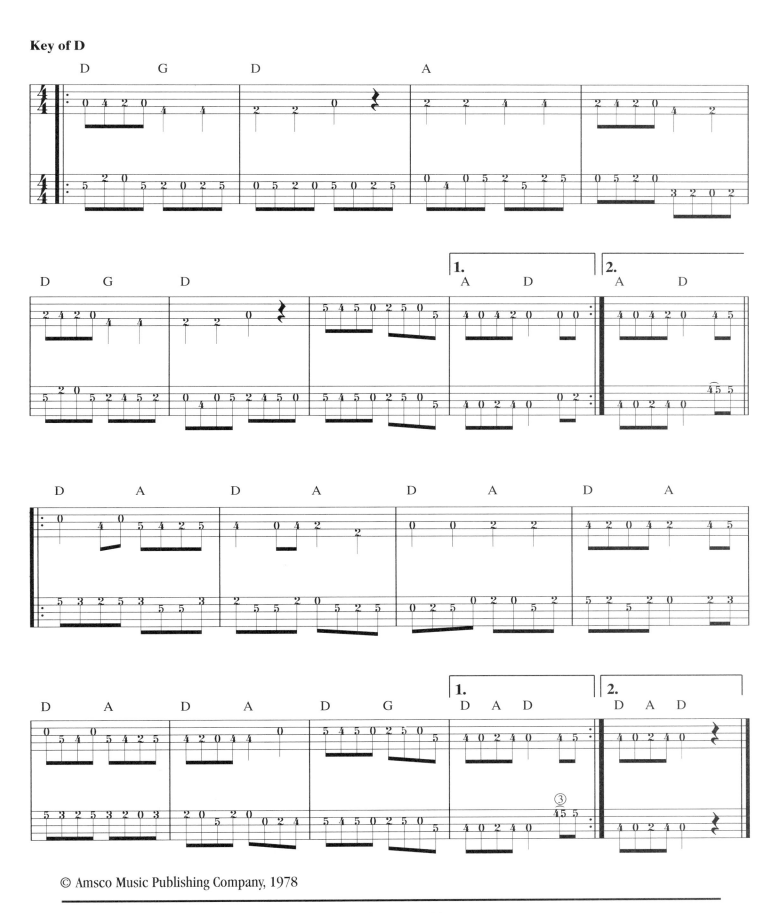

The next few tunes are in the key of G. The following G scale will help you with the fingering.

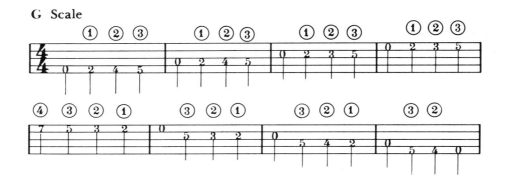

Little Maggie

John Hardy

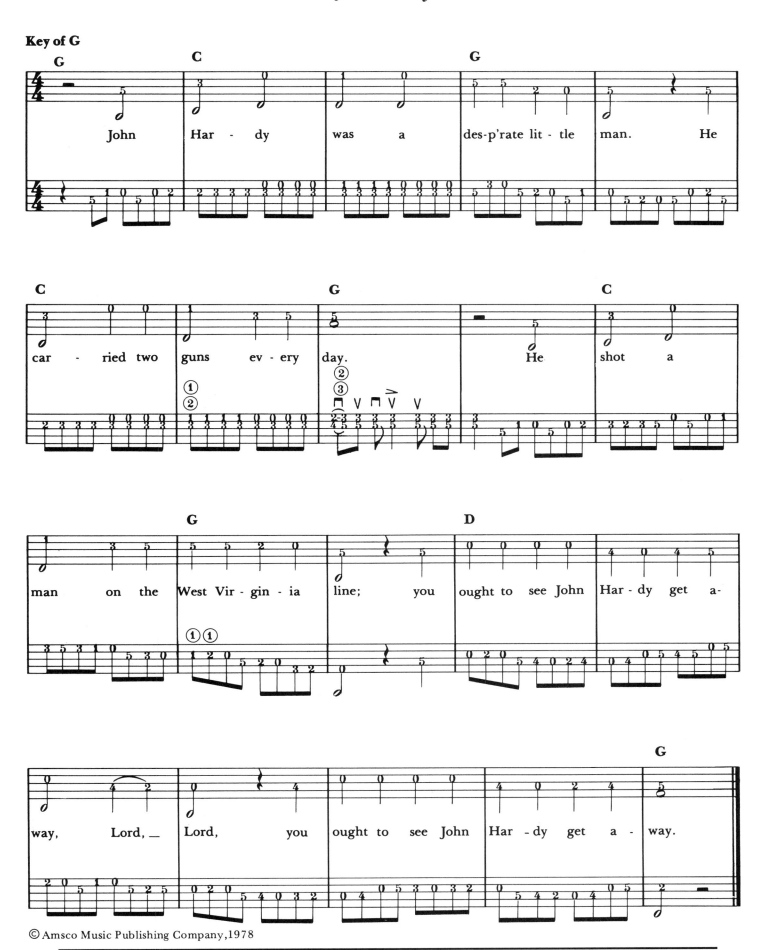

This song will be tough on your pinky. The lead-in to the second part of the solo can be played with the index finger fretting both the A and D strings.

Enjoy the different chords in the rhythmic accompaniment section.

Blackberry Blossom

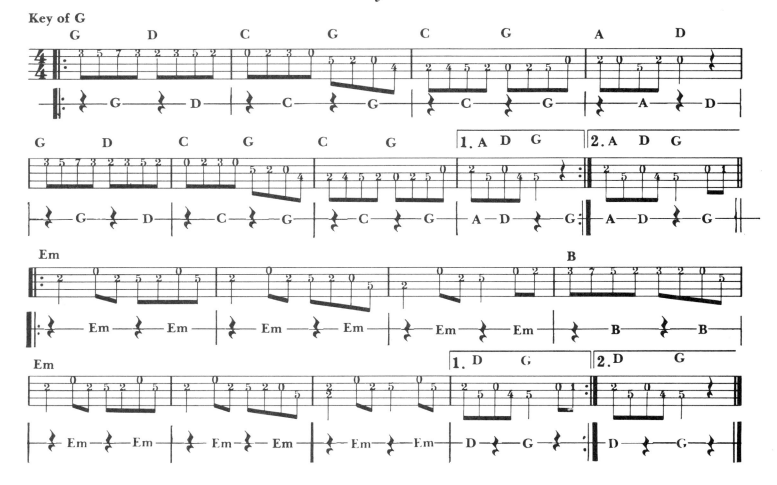

Blackberry Blossom

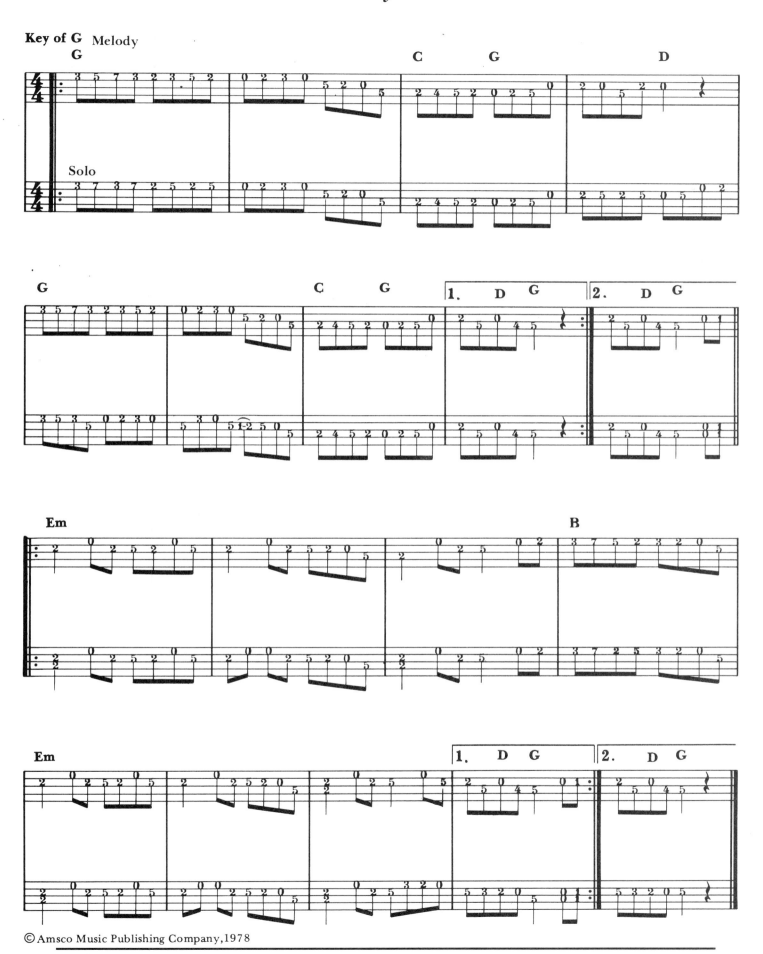

The fingering for the second part of the solo is difficult. The following example will help you with it.

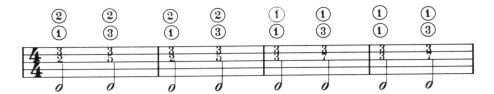

Turkey in the Straw

This bawdy tune has typical ragtime chord changes to spice it up.

Salty Dog

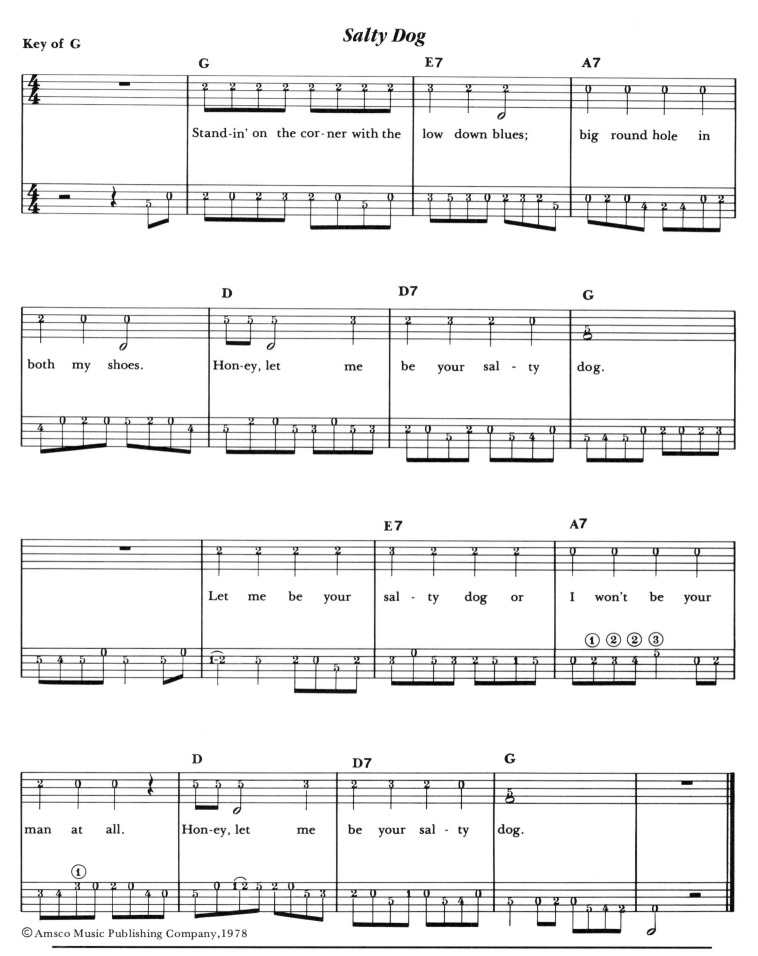

Sitting on Top of the World

Key of A

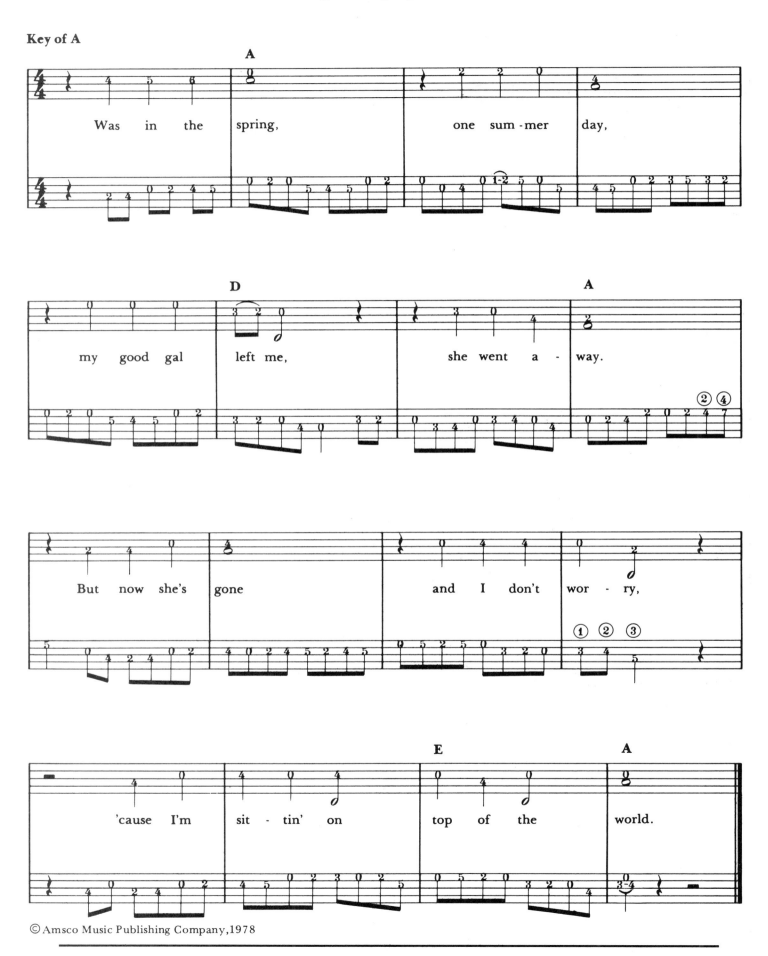

Was in the spring, one sum-mer day, my good gal left me, she went a - way.

But now she's gone and I don't wor - ry, 'cause I'm sit - tin' on top of the world.

Pretty Polly

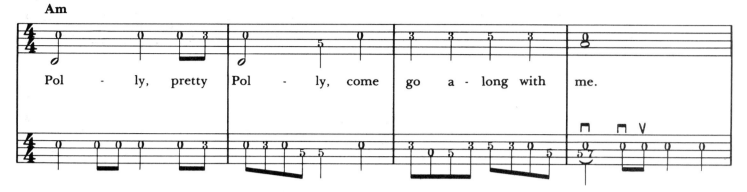

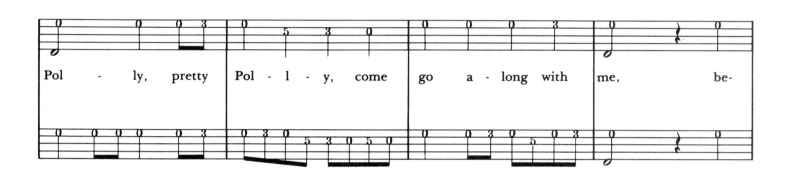

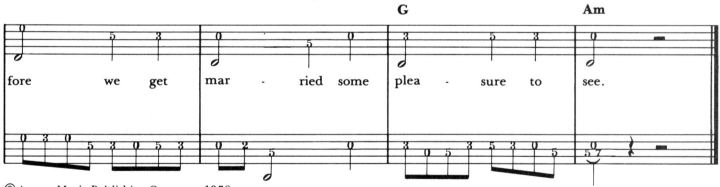

Patty on the Turnpike

Key of G

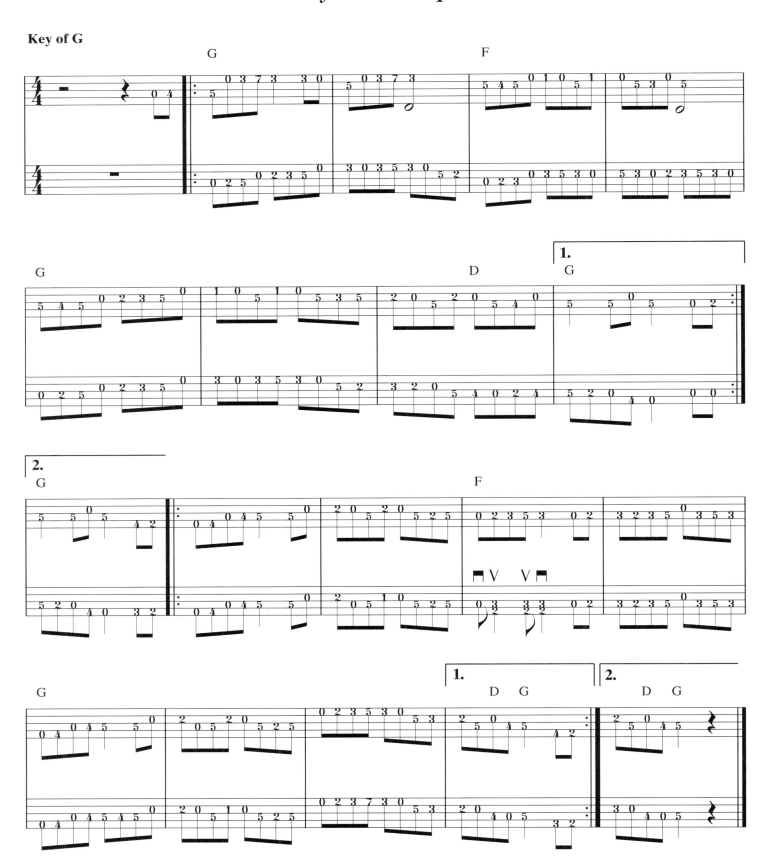

The first pull-off we find is in *Stoney Point.* A down-stroke is used to hit the first string, which is fretted at the third fret. After the string rings, pluck it rapidly in succession as follows: the second finger of the left hand plucks the E string at the third fret while the first finger frets it at the second fret. Then the first finger plucks the E string at the second fret. All this is done within the space of a quarter note.

Pull-offs aren't easy. They will hurt your fingertips at first, but you'll eventually build up thicker calluses and strengthen your fingers.

Stoney Point

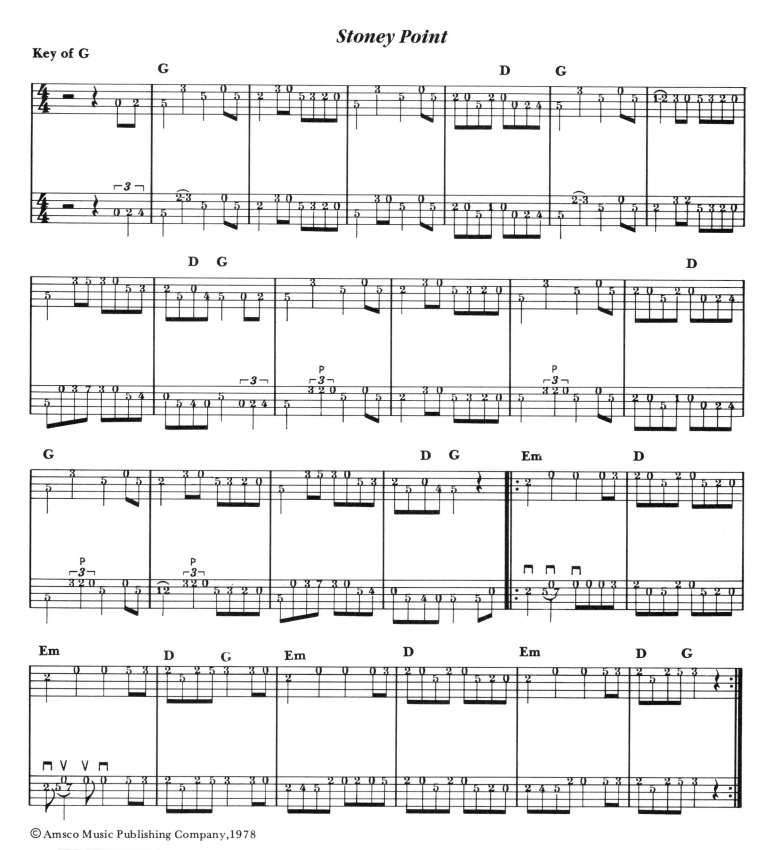

John Henry

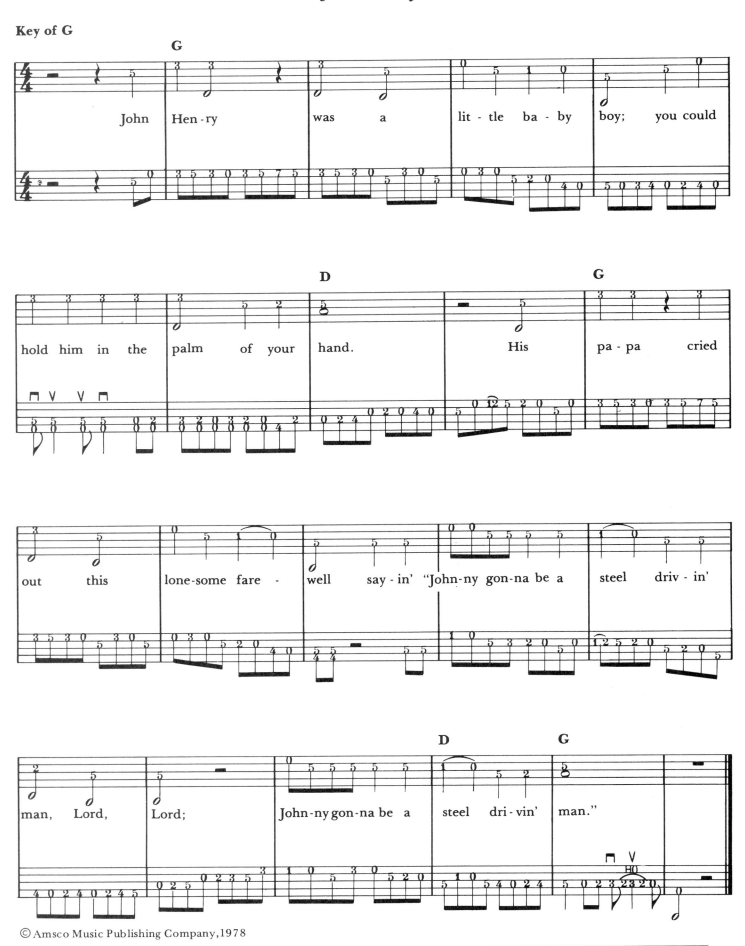

These next two tunes introduce the use of tremolo. To begin with, you might play just the melody, using a tremolo. After you know the melody, move on to the solo. Don't let the harmonies confuse you.

The tremolo is played continuously between two tied tremolo notes. The following is an example of this:

The dotted quarter notes equal three eighth notes.

The dotted half notes equal three quarter notes.

All the Good Times Are Past and Gone

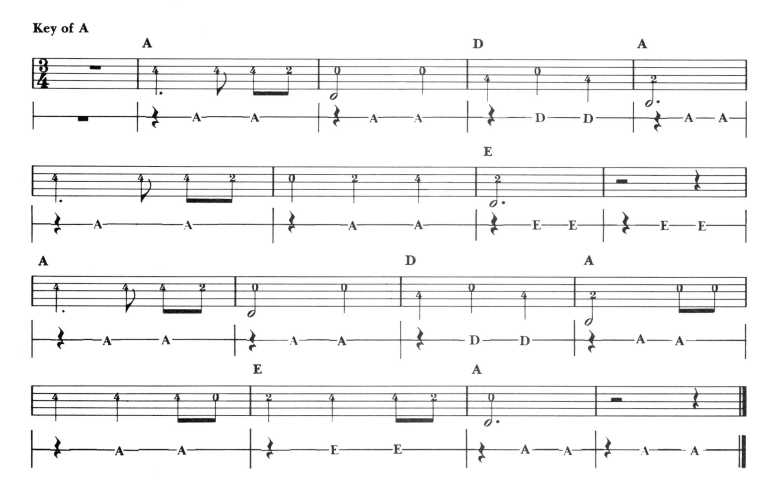

All the Good Times Are Past and Gone

Key of A

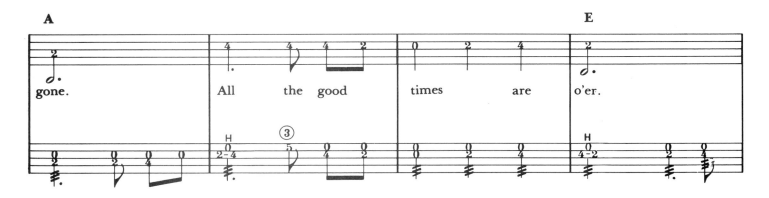

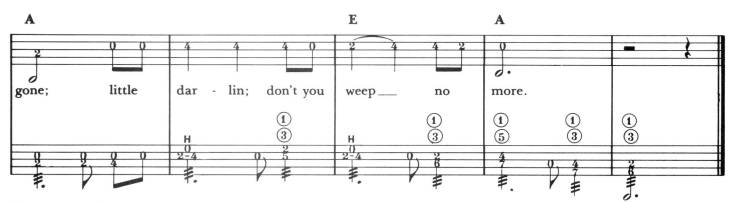

Will the Circle Be Unbroken

Key of D

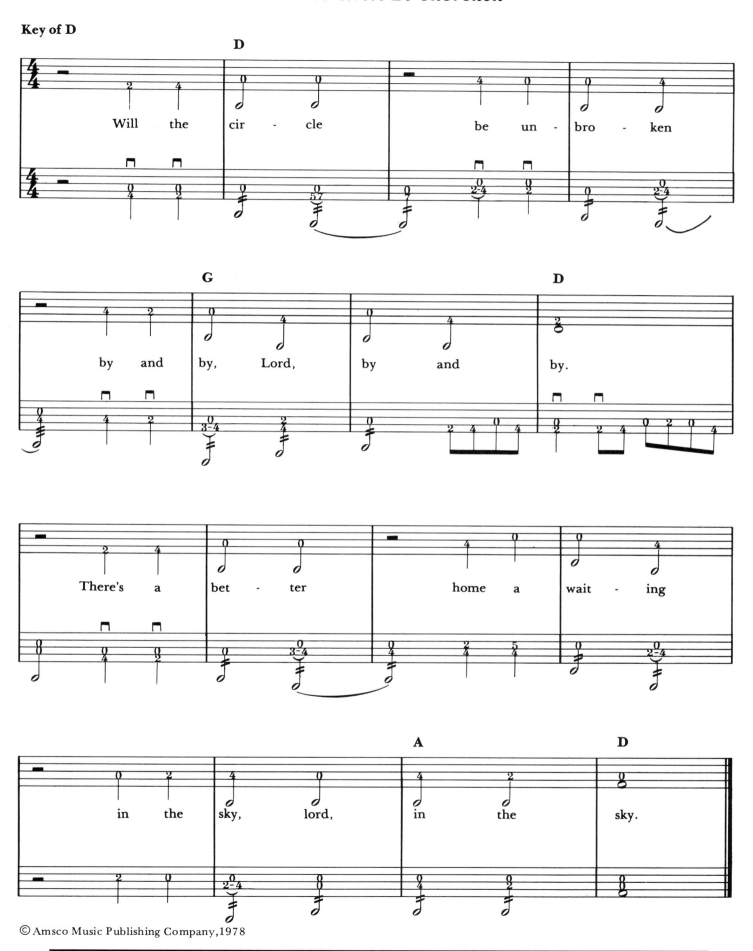

Playing Octaves and the Osborne Shuffle

Now that your fingers are gaining some strength and dexterity, let's learn two new interesting techniques. The first of these will be playing octaves.

In recent years more and more bluegrass mandolinists have been using octaves in their playing. Try the following example. It's not easy, and it will require some effort at first. However, after a few days' practice your fingers will be able to make and hold the necessary stretch. Be sure not to overtax your fingers. When they get tired, stop and rest. Shake your hand and fingers rapidly. This will relax them and send blood to nourish your tired muscles. Make sure the pinky and index finger are fretting the notes cleanly. When you move the octave, check to see that you're playing the correct notes.

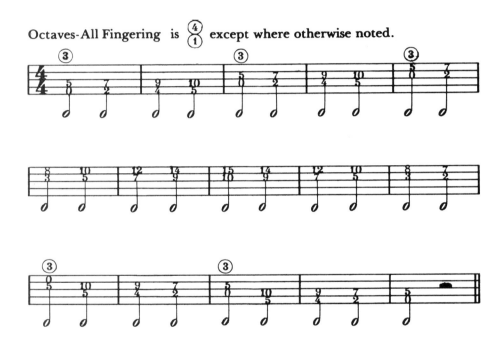

You now see how octaves are formed and moved. Let's put them to use. Octaves naturally lend themselves to a jazzy type of phrasing. This will become apparent in the next song. Follow the rhythms carefully.

Nine Pound Hammer

Key of G

Now that you understand octaves, let's move on. The next tune uses an adapted version of what is known as a double shuffle on the fiddle. Its use on mandolin was introduced by Bobby Osborne and is sometimes referred to as the *Osborne Shuffle.* It is done on two adjacent strings. One unchanging, low drone note alternates with several higher notes. This is done to a special rhythmic pattern, which is as follows:

Now that you understand the rhythm, let's add some more notes:

As you can see, this moving pattern creates a nifty sound. Let's see it in action.

Devil's Dream

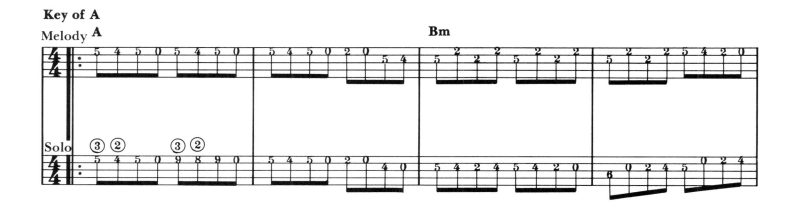

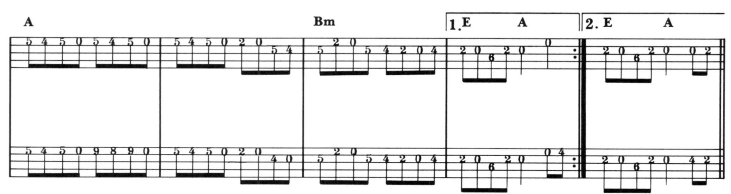

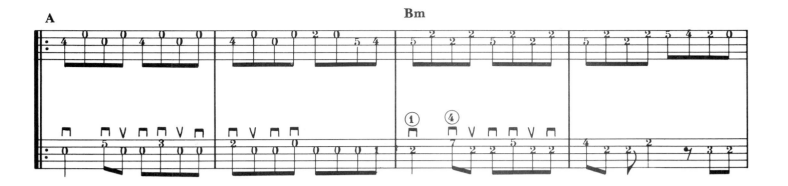

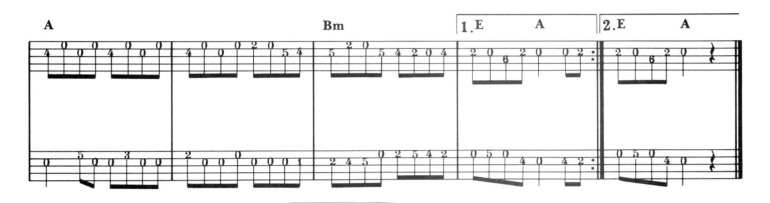

More Advanced Tunes

The next three fiddle tunes are more advanced. Consult the A scale to help you with the fingerings in *Durham's Reel*. The following B scale will help you understand the proper way to play over the B chord in this tune.

This scale can be moved up and down the neck to any key. Try this next exercise using the same fingering as in the one above.

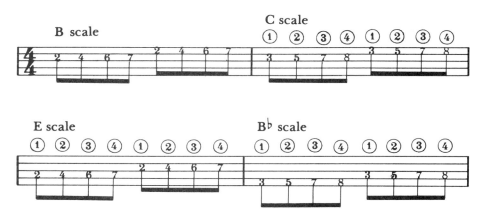

Fire on the Mountain

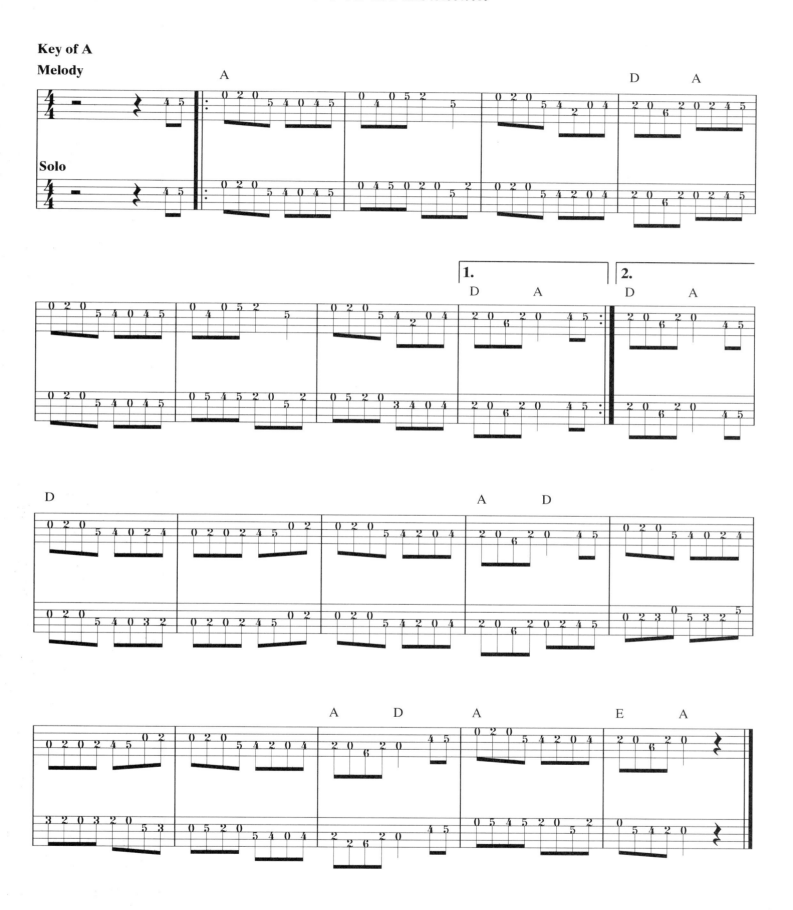

Durham's Reel

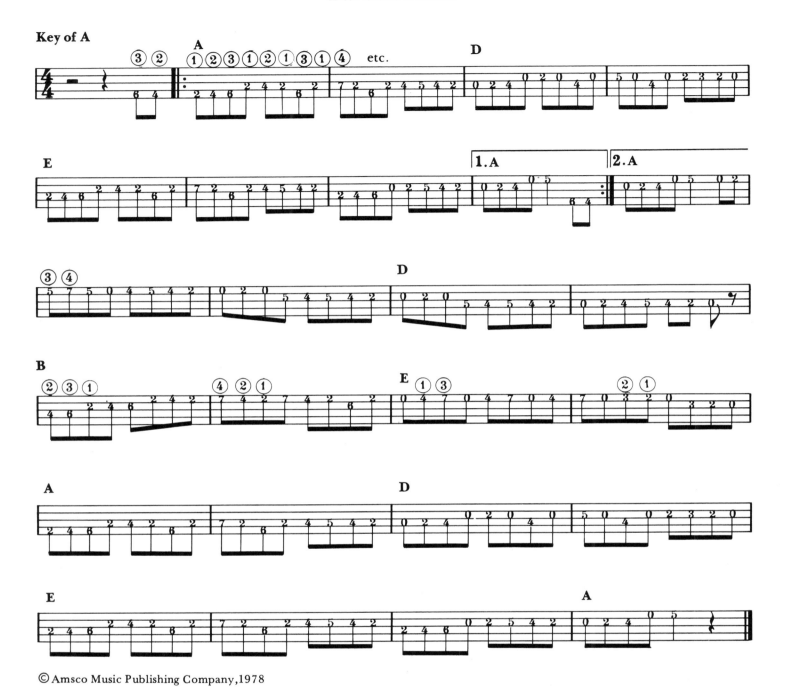

Done Gone is a three-part tune in B-flat. It's a tough one, but well worth the effort.

Done Gone

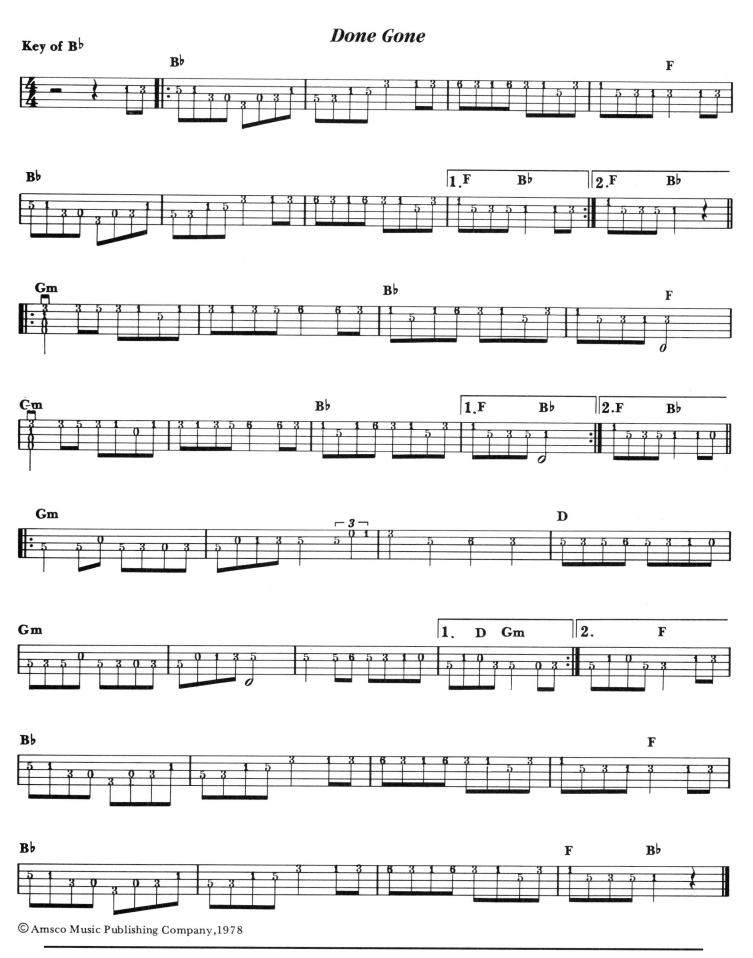

Double Stops

A double stop consists of two notes played together at the same time. Double stops are formed by simple positions on the neck. Like chords, they can be formed in any key if the position is moved to the appropriate fret.

Here are three basic double stop positions. They're in the key of G. Try to play them.

Key of G

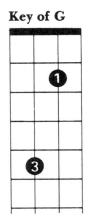
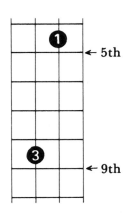
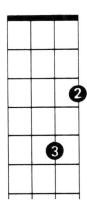

Now try the same position in the key of B.

Key of B

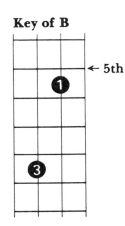
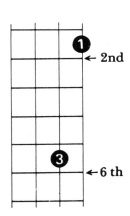
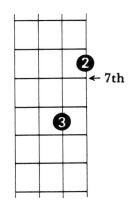

Position I can be played on the middle two strings at the ninth and thirteenth frets; however, it's easier to play it at the second and sixth frets on the first and second strings.

These three positions always follow one another on the neck in an ascending or descending order. For example, if you start ascending with position I, it will be followed by positions II and III. If you start ascending with position II, it will be followed by positions III and I. Position III is followed by positions I and II. In actual playing, it's not necessary to follow this consecutive order. Feel free to move from one position to another.

The following two charts will show you these positions in the keys of G and C. As previously mentioned, move them to the appropriate fret for each different key.

Some Doublestops in the Key of G

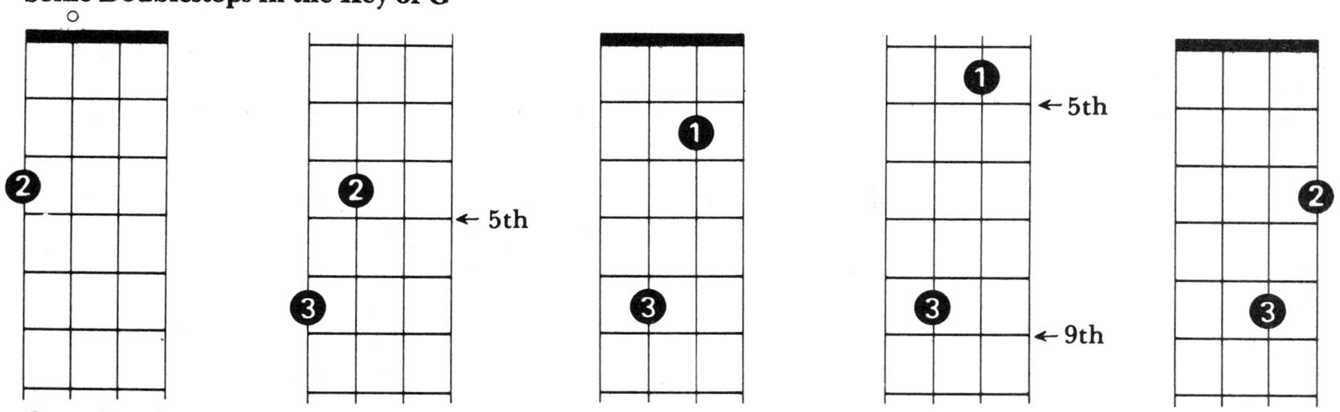

Open D string
is played

Basic Doublestops in the Key of C

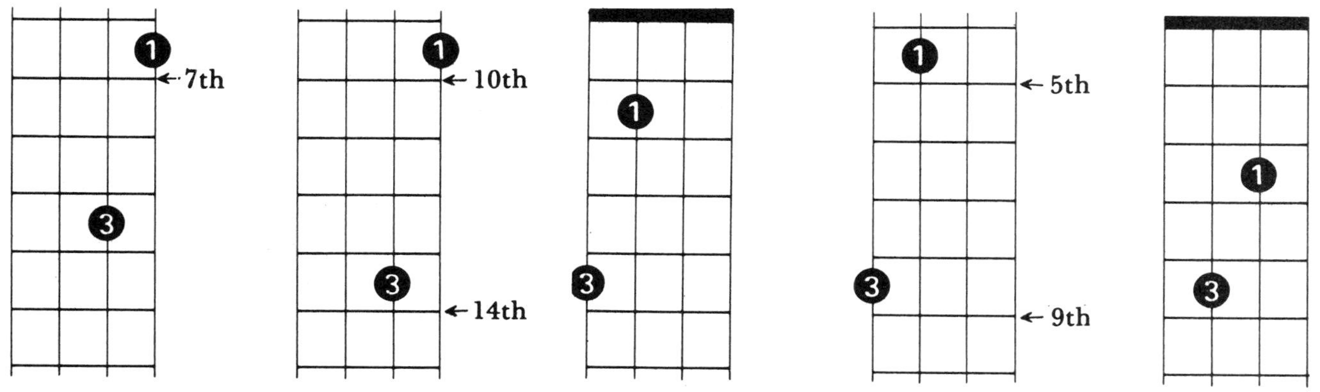

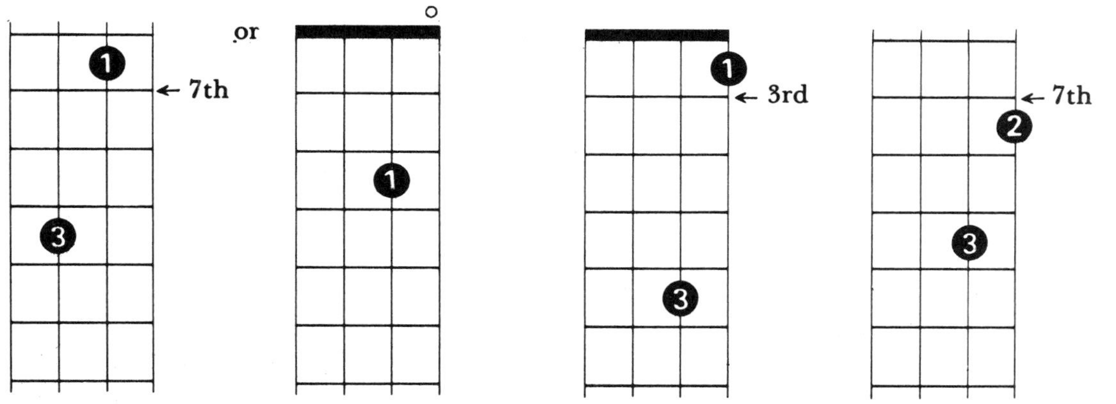

or

Open E string
Is played

Double stops can be used in any tune. They are especially effective in slow, tremoloed songs, supplying a pretty harmony to the lead. Learn the double stops in all the different keys. They will give you a greater knowledge of the fingerboard and thus improve your playing. Experiment with them to see where they sound and feel best.

Crosspicking

The big breakthrough in banjo playing in the mid-1940s was the development of the three-finger right-hand pattern or roll. Earl Scruggs was its foremost exponent. It's this three-finger roll (three fingers alternately picking the strings) that gives bluegrass banjo its distinctive sound.

Jesse McReynolds, a mandolin player from Virginia, decided to try and adapt this sound to the mandolin. He developed a roll using a flat pick instead of three fingers. This style became known as crosspicking. A similar but less developed technique was occasionally used by the hot tenor banjo players of the 1920s and 1930s.

Jesse had to develop a whole new series of left-hand positions to work with this roll. This sometimes meant playing a note on a lower string high up on the neck, instead of at the third or fourth fret on a higher string. This is not as difficult as it may sound, and the results are incredibly exciting.

Let's begin by learning the basic roll. The roll in its simplest form is played like this:

1) third string, down-stroke

2) first string, up-stroke

3) second string, up-stroke

In actual playing, though, you'll usually combine two of these patterns with an additional down-up stroke to form your basic roll. It looks like this: down-up-up-down-up-up-down-up.

In every two bars of the following exercise the last down-up changes from the third and first strings to the third and second strings. Don't get confused. Play these eighth notes smoothly and evenly.

This roll can be expanded into the following monster: down-up-up-down-up-up-down-up-up-down-up-down-up-up-down-up. Let's put this to use:

At this point you may notice that the fingers of your right hand tend to move with each note. This is natural. Crosspicking is a style based on finger movement. Some players brace their third and fourth fingers in front of the bridge and move the pick with their index finger and thumb. The wrist is left loose, and complements the finger motion. On the down-stroke, the thumb presses down and the index finger moves freely along with it. On the up-stroke, the index finger pushes up and the thumb responds.

Think of crosspicking as a smooth flow of notes, not as single notes grouped together. Get into a flow.

Bile 'Em Cabbage Down shows a typical McReynolds break in the keys of A and G.

In *Swing Low* we find another McReynolds break, this time in the key of B. Learn the following positions. The break centers around them:

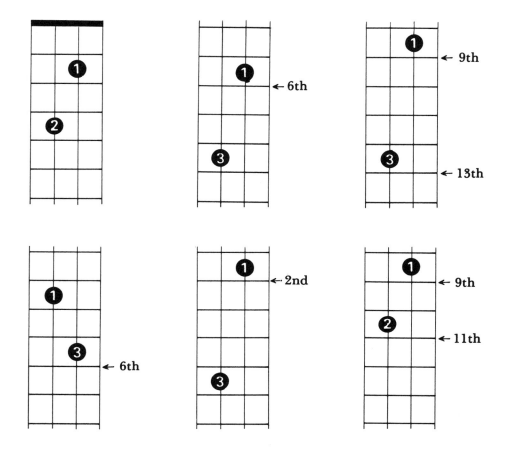

Bile 'Em Cabbage Down

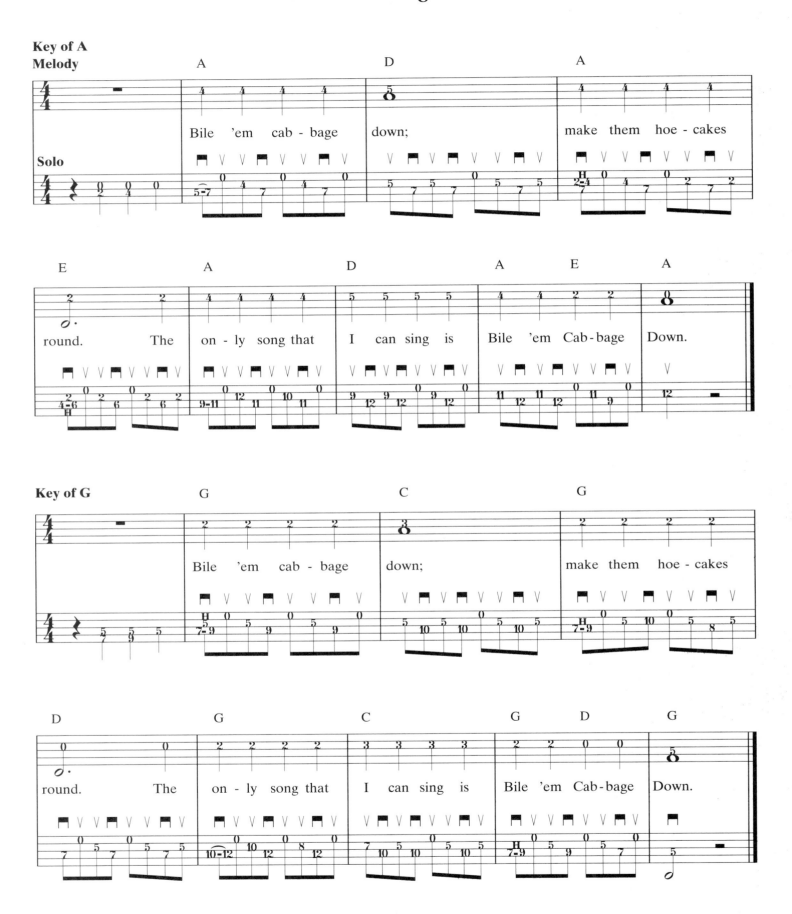

Swing Low

Discography

One of the best ways to get your playing together is to listen to the pros. They'll show you what to do and when to do it. Listen, enjoy, and learn. When you find a solo you like, tune your mandolin to the track, and try to figure it out. This will be difficult at first, but with practice, your ear will develop and it will become easier to do.

I know of players who figured out every solo they could get their hands on. You don't have to be quite this dedicated, but the importance of learning from recordings can't be stressed enough. It will increase your catalogue of tunes, give you new ideas, and teach you new techniques. Professional recordings are real examples of what to do.

Now, which recordings to buy? Hmm, this one has a nice cover. Oh, such a lusty lass on the cover of that one! Ah, this cover has such a pleasant barnyard scene. Yeah! Those devilish lads in cowboy hats and western attire on the cover, I'll buy it! Yes... I'll buy it!

Wrong. Don't be misled by a fancy cover. It's what's inside that counts. I do believe that some people are in tune and can tell whether the recording is good or bad by its vibe, but not all of us are quite that far along on the path.

That is where this list comes in. Check out these sides. They're brimming with just the stuff you want!

Bill Monroe

Monroe, the father of bluegrass, made records for sixty years. Most of the sides listed here were recorded for Decca in the 1950s and 1960s. In the 1970s, Decca was taken over by MCA which continues to release most of their albums.

I Saw the Light (MCA CS-527)
Recorded in the early 1950s, this gospel recording features vocal quartets and the lead singing of the great Ed Mayfield. It is considered to be one of Monroe's best. His mandolin playing is full of unusual and exciting ideas.

Country Music Hall of Fame (MCA CD-10082)

16 All Time Greatest Hits (CBS 01065)

Bill Monroe & His Bluegrass Boys: Live Recordings 1956-69 (Smithsonian Folkways 40063)
This is a great collection of material from the beginning of the folk boom when Monroe began using some great, young, northern-born musicians.

Bill Monroe & Doc Watson: Live Recordings 1963-80 (Smithsonian Folkways 40064)
Just a mandolin, a guitar, and two voices; Bill and Doc are in great form—the roots of bluegrass.

The Essential Bill Monroe 1945-1949 (Columbia C2K-52478)
The Flatt and Scruggs years, this is the blueprint for all bluegrass bands that followed.

Bluegrass 1950-1958 (Bear Family BCD-15423)

Bluegrass 1959-1969 (Bear Family BCD-11529-4)
These two box sets have it all! Four CDs in chronological order and a great booklet.

Jim and Jesse McReynolds

Jim & Jesse:1952-1955 (Bear Family CD-15635)

Music Among Friends (Rounder CD-0279)

Shelton Special: Alan Shelton (Rounder RR0088)

Y'All Come: The Essential Jim & Jesse (Legacy/Epic Country Classics 65076)
The above recordings feature Jesse in several settings. Shelton Special, has some fine examples of Jesse's playing.

The Osborne Brothers

Bobby Osborne developed an exciting mandolin style that opened up many new possibilities and gave a greater freedom to the mandolin player. This style consisted of an even flow of eighth- and sixteenth- notes and was adapted from fiddle playing. Much of what was to follow is based on his style. The Osborne Brothers feature some of the best singing and picking around. Unfortunately, many of the great records they recorded for Decca in the 1960s are out of print.

The Best of the Osborne Brothers (Sugar Hill 2203)

The Class of '96 (Pine Castle 1059)
This is a good, modern recording and features some fine younger players like Terry Eldridge.

Frank Wakefield

Frank Wakefield is one of the most inventive players on the scene.
Frank absorbed the influence of Monroe, Osborne, and McReynolds
and developed a style all his own. His high-powered playing served as the model for many mandolinists.

with Red Allen
The Kitchen Tapes (Acoustic Disc ACD-11)
This recording is literally Red and Frank sitting around the kitchen table and playing in the most relaxed setting imaginable. Both are in top form, and without the clutter of a full band you can really hear all the great mandolin that Frank's playing. Solos, backup, and a great chop—Frank's got it all.

The Country Gentlemen

Folk Songs Old & New (Smithsonian Folkways CD-SF 40004)

Folk Songs & Bluegrass (Smithsonian Folkways CD-SF 40022)
These recordings are by the great band of the late 1950s and mid- 1960s. John Duffy, a highly original player, is heard on both. His hot style added new dimensions to mandolin playing. In the late 1960s he formed the Seldom Scene, and can be heard on their records.

In recent years the impeccable stylings of Jimmy Gadreau and Doyle Lawson have graced the Gentlemen's records.

Sam Bush

Sam is a trendsetter. He's the foremost exponent of what is called New Grass. His powerful, even style shows the influence of Texas fiddle music and rock and roll.

with New Grass Revival
New Grass Revival (Capitol 35161)

Fly Through the Country (Flying Fish FF70032)

David Grisman

Dave is one of the greats. A protégé of Frank Wakefield and an A1 student of bluegrass mandolin. Dave was turning heads around as early as the mid-1960s; and, after several years of playing rock and roll, bluegrass, doing studio work and composing, Dave formed a quintet which centered around his many talents. The quintet features extended improvisations in which David's jazzy and soulful mandolin soars. He is also a great teacher.

The David Grisman Rounder Album (Rounder 0069)

The David Grisman Quintet (Rhino 71468)

with Bill Keith
Something Auld, Something Newgrass, Something Borrowed, Something Bluegrass (Rounder 0084)

with Jerry Garcia, Vassar Clements, and Peter Rowan
Old & in the Way (Arista 14022)

with Don Stover
Things in Life (Rounder 0014)

Andy Statman

Ah, yes. A chance to toot my own horn... I mean mandolin. I play in a style considered unorthodox and avant-garde by some; however, my playing is steeped in the bluegrass tradition. I've been influenced by jazz, rhythm and blues, Balkan and Middle Eastern music. My style introduces new rhythmic and harmonic concepts to bluegrass.

with Tony Trischka
Bluegrass Light (Rounder 0048)
Heartlands (Rounder 0062)

Both of these recordings have been re-released on a single CD:
The Early Years (Rounder 11578)

with Vassar Clements
Bluegrass Sessions (Flying Fish FF038)

There is not enough space to talk about all the great mandolinists. Some of them not discussed are listed below. Don't neglect to listen and learn from them.

Red Rector
Has recorded several excellent instrumental albums.

with Authentic Band
Mountain Music Bluegrass Style (Smithsonian Folkways 2318)

Roland White
Played with the Kentucky Colonels, Lester Flatt, Bill Monroe, and Country Gazette.
Appalachian Swing (Rounder SS31)

Hershel Sizemore
Has recorded with The Dixie Gentlemen, Vassar Clements, The Shenandoah Cutups and Rural Yarborough.

The following records are not bluegrass but will be of interest to any mandolin player:

Jethro Burns
Jethro is the jazz mandolinist.

Bye, Bye Blues (Acoustic Disc ACD-26)

Swing Low, Sweet Mandolin (Acoustic Disc ACD-15)

Dave Apollon
A technical wizard, Apollon plays standards and eastern European folk tunes with passion.

Man with the Mandolin (Acoustic Disc ACD-27)

Tiny Moore
Recorded with Bob Wills, Merle Haggard, and Johnny Gimble. He plays perhaps the finest western swing and bebop mandolin on a five-string electric.

Jacob Bittencourt
This excellent mandolinist (called Bandolim in Brazil) plays beautiful sambas and Brazilian tunes. In his country he is known as Jacob do Bandolim.

a.k.a. Jacob Do Bandolim
Original Classic Recordings, Vol. 1: Mandolin Master of Brazil (Acoustic Disc ACD-3)
Original Classic Recordings, Vol. 2 (Acoustic Disc ACD-13)

Johnny Young
Excellent Chicago blues mandolinist. He has recorded on several labels.

Harry Reser
Unbelievable flatpicking, original tunes, and an excellent technique. This recording will provide a wealth of ideas for the mandolinist.

Banjo Crackerjax (Yazoo1048)

Bibliography

Tottle, Jack. *Bluegrass Mandolin*. New York: Oak Publications, 1975.
Good follow-up to this book. Goes into greater detail.

Wernick, Peter. *Bluegrass Songbook*. New York: Oak Publications, 1976.
Contains a wealth of material, along with many tips from the greats of bluegrass.

Chord Charts

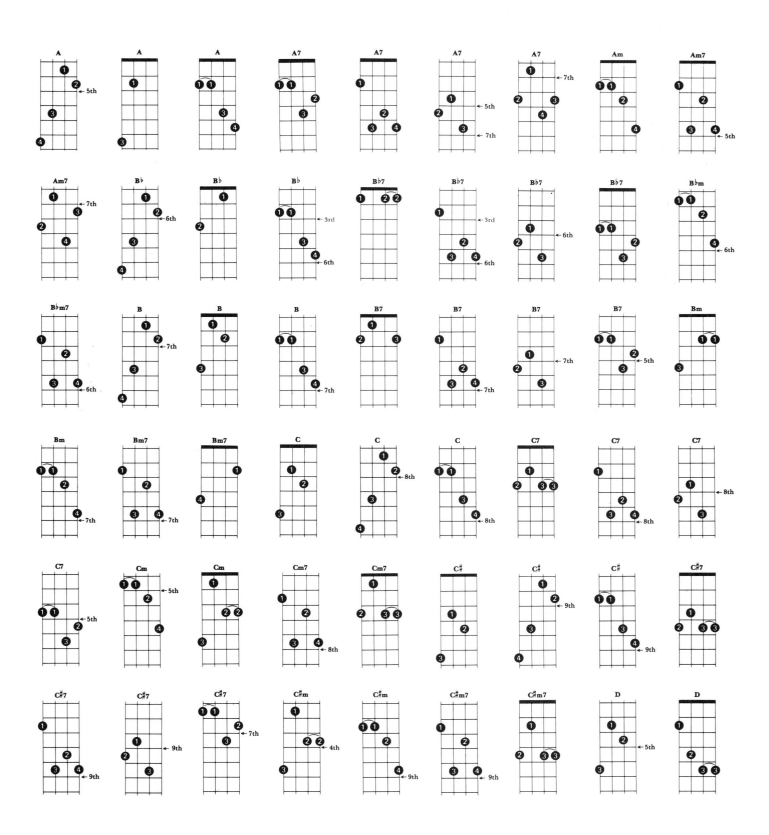

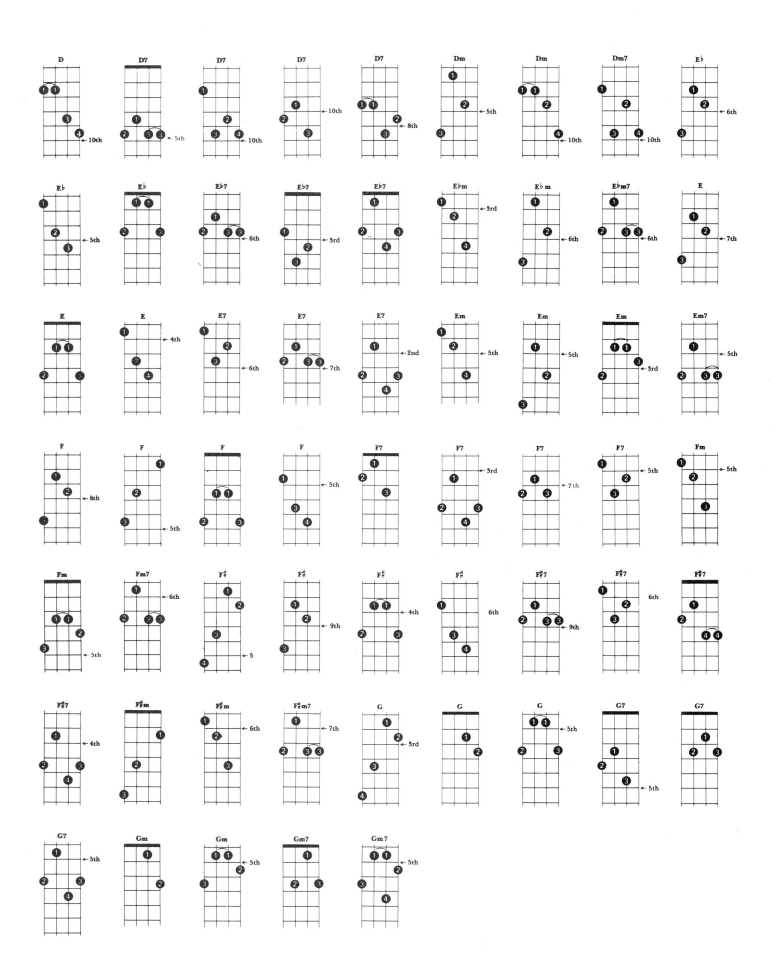